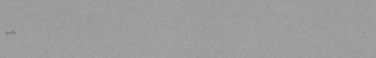

ANIMAL shark DIARIES

STEVE PARKER

QED

First published in the UK in 2012 by
QED Publishing
A Quarto Group company
230 City Road
London EC1V 2TT
www.qed-publishing.co.uk

A catalogue record for this book is available from the British Library.

ISBN 978 1 84835 844 7

Editor Carey Scott
Illustrator Peter David Scott/The Art Agency
Designer Dave Ball

Printed and bound in China

Picture Credits
Key: t = top, b = bottom, l = left, r = right, c = centre,
FC = front cover, BC = back cover.
Corbis Jeffrey Rotman 24 b, 27 t; **Getty** Reinhard Dirscherl 13 t; **Nature** 5 t,
Shutterstock Grafica 11 tl, John A. Anderson p12 t, Zacarias Pereira de Mata
p18 t, Maksimilian p20 b, Gordan, David M. Scrader, Luminis, Oleg Golovnev,
Ana de Sousa, Valentin Agapov, Dementeva, Petr Jilek all background images

Contents

check out my totally unique head!

Hello World!

Today I swam past Seaweed Garden into The Shallows. It's the first place I remember, because it's where I was born. There I saw new baby sharks with their mother. It brought back memories of when I was a 'pup', as we sharks call our babies.

Female bumps male before mating.

Male twists around female.

I quickly learned that sharks, like most fish, are not caring parents. My brothers, sisters and I had to learn to swim and hunt all on our own. Some of them got eaten by other fish - even other sharks.

Each pup is about 50 centimetres long.

4

But I survived and I'm growing fast - soon I'll be old enough to make pups of my own. Senior Shark told me all about that. Everyone likes Senior Shark, who knows everything but is still quite friendly. Respect!

Empty shark egg cases are known as 'mermaid's purses'.

The yolk is a store of food for the baby.

Senior says that not all kinds of sharks have babies. Some lay eggs in tough cases, which they leave on the sea bed. Inside the case, the egg grows into a pup, using the yolk as food. Finally it bites its way out: 'Hello World!'

Tendrils attach the egg case to rocks and weeds.

Pups quickly learn to swish their tails and swim.

Big-Head

Now I'm about half-grown, I am trying new food. I've learned to find flat fish like skates and rays. They lie on the seabed and their colours blend in. This is known as camouflage. Sometimes they bury themselves in the sand and stones. I track them down using my super-senses!

Our wide, flat heads are totally unique!

My mouth skin is especially sensitive.

Our skin feels water currents and temperature.

My strange head shape might look funny but it's actually really useful! My eyes can see a wider view than other sharks. My nostrils are wide apart too, so I'm good at detecting smells that come from the side.

Manta the ray has a weird head too! Her paddle-like mouth parts steer water into her mouth. She feeds by filtering tiny creatures called ~~planktun~~ plankton from the water.

Manta swims by flapping her wide, wing-like pectoral fins.

My nostril is at the end of my hammer lobe.

Tiny pits on my head help me to locate prey.

Manta's paddles guide water into her huge mouth.

I've got a special sense, which Senior Shark calls the electrosense. Small pits or holes on my head feel the natural electrical signals given off by the muscles of other creatures. This helps me to find prey - even in the dark!

WHAT I DID TODAY

1. Swam with Manta.

2. Caught a fish and ate it.

3. Swam with Manta again.

4. Caught another fish.

The Bay

I grew up with my brothers and sisters in the quiet waters of The Bay. I've got to know all the rocky caves, sunken boats and other secret places there. If bigger fish come to hunt us, I quickly swim away to hide in one of them.

The tail is our caudal fin.

Front side fins are pectorals.

I'm better at swimming, compared to when I was a pup. Now I can turn around without tipping over sideways. It sounds simple, but controlling eight fins is a tough task!

Our rear side fins are pelvics.

The Bay has small fish and shellfish for us to eat. When mackerel shoals arrive, I like to eat the youngsters. Baby squid and octopus are tasty too, although a bit slippery. Crabs and shrimps are... crunchy!

Smooth Hammerhead

Group Fish – Sharks

Adult length Up to 5 metres

Weight Up to 400 kilogrammes

Habitat Warm to cool seas and oceans, especially near coasts

Food Fish, including other sharks and rays, also squid, octopus, shellfish such as crabs and shrimps

Features Wide head shaped like a flat hammer, eyes and nostrils at the ends of the hammer lobes

Senior Shark's front dorsal was bitten, ouch!

Wrecked boats are great hiding places.

Here's my tooth test!

Today I bit my diary page so I could count my teeth. I've got about 30. Senior Shark has more than 50. Sharp!

In the Swim

Long ago, when I was small, I swam out towards Deep Reef. It was strange to have so much empty water all around. The water was cooler too, and I soon got tired. So I came back to the warm shallows near the coast.

The more I swish my tail, the faster I swim.

Like most sharks, I have to keep moving all the time, or I would sink.

I often forget to use my anal fin.

THINGS TO REMEMBER WHEN SWIMMING

1. Swish tail sideways.

2. Angle head slightly up.

3. Tilt pectorals to turn.

4. Slant dorsals to lean over.

5. Stay alert for dangers, such as bigger sharks, anchors and boats.

Today I'll head out to Wide-Open Ocean for a while, to practise my swimming. I find that shark fins are quite stiff. We cannot twist and turn as quickly as other fish. They have bendy fins, even some that fold up or spread out like a fan.

LEARNING TO USE FINS

First, move just one fin, to see how it affects your swimming. Try this with each fin in turn. Then you can begin to alter two fins at a time, followed by three, and so on.

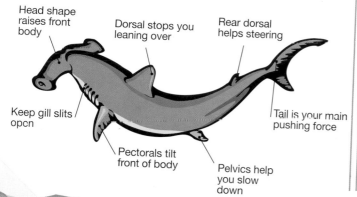

Head shape raises front body

Dorsal stops you leaning over

Rear dorsal helps steering

Keep gill slits open

Tail is your main pushing force

Pectorals tilt front of body

Pelvics help you slow down

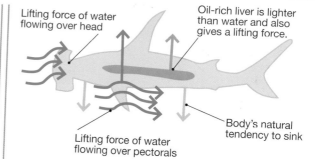

Lifting force of water flowing over head

Oil-rich liver is lighter than water and also gives a lifting force.

Lifting force of water flowing over pectorals

Body's natural tendency to sink

GOING UP AND DOWN

As a shark, you lack the swim bladder that other fish have, which enables them to rise and sink. But you have a huge liver (part of your digestive system) filled with tiny oil drops. These are lighter than water to help your buoyancy, or floating ability.

My side muscles are very strong.

My Shark Skills manual is a great help. It shows me how to use my different fins. It also explains how my strange head shape actually helps me to stop sinking. As water flows over and under it, my front end is pushed up with a lifting force. So it stops me from nose-diving. Neat!

My pectorals are best for steering.

Without my head shape, fast swimming would be more tiring.

Neighbours

Being a shark can be quite lonely. I like to chat to other creatures, but when I swim near, they often hide or race away. I don't want to eat all of them. Just one or two, and only now and then.

Octo can be bright red, green and in-between.

Crab can scuttle around quickly on her eight legs.

Eight-armed Octo is truly amazing. He can change shape and colour in a flash. He's a Caribbean reef octopus and hunts mainly at night. I've eaten octopus a few times - very chewy.

There are many kinds of crunchy crabs all over Rocky Reef. Atlantic blue crabs are just a snack for me. I try and bite them from behind so they don't pinch my mouth.

Conch's hard shell is too much trouble for me to crack open.

Conch is one kind of seasnail. Like Octo, she's a type of creature called a ~~mullose~~ mollusc.

Conch emerging from her shell.

Big Mack is the biggest in our local shoal of king mackerel. He's a terrific hunter. I've learned some useful tips from watching him catch small fish.

Like the other starfish at Rocky Reef, Red-Cushion Seastar has 5 arms.

I just don't see the point of starfish. They have no brains, no proper eyes, and they are sooooo slow! But there are thousands of them on Rocky Reef. They smother and eat sponges, corals and small creatures like worms and shellfish.

BIG MACK: FRIEND OR ENEMY?

1. King mackerel are sometimes friends. They chase small fish towards me.

2. King mackerel can be enemies. They steal fish I want to eat.

3. King mackerel are predators and prey too. Big ones eat baby sharks, and I eat small mackerel!

Nasty Noise

BOAT RACE SIGNALS DANGER FOR THE BAY

An unusual above-surface view by our aerial photographer Albert Ross

Calling all fish and other sea creatures: tomorrow is the most dangerous day of the year in The Bay. Horrid boats and ships of all shapes and sizes will be racing to and fro. There will be noisy, churning motorboats with whirling propellers, silent yachts with deep, sharp hulls, and skimming water-skiers who keep falling in. All sea animals are warned to hide away or leave for the day. Safety Officer Sandy Squid, of The Bay Shelter Patrol, has this advice:

• Starfish – slide under the nearest stone.
• Seasnails – withdraw into your shells.
• Crabs – burrow under the sand.
• Jellyfish – because you swim so weakly, you should have left already, as we advised last week.
• Worms and shrimps – dig down into the mud.
• Small fish – look for cracks and crevices among the rocks.
• Big fish including sharks – head out to deeper water.

The speedboat's propeller makes a deafening noise.

My senses are distorted by the waves.

Every year there's a huge and deadly event in The Bay. Ships and boats rush about like crazy. What are they doing? Beats me. But I do know that each year, several of my friends get hit and hurt, or even killed. This year it was poor old Manny.

Manny has been hurt but is struggling on.

Pressure waves push us around.

Manny is the most peaceful creature I know. But a speedboat's propeller made terrible cuts on her back. After detecting blood from far away, some sharks might gather around and ... you know. But everyone loves Manny. So we're leaving her alone, in the hope she will recover.

West Indian Manatee

Group Mammals – Sea-cows

Adult length Up to 4 metres

Weight Up to 1200 kilogrammes

Habitat Shallow waters along coasts, lagoons and rivers

Food Sea grass and other plants, also some small fish, worms and other creatures

Features Bendy, whiskery snout, front flippers, large paddle-shaped tail

So Many Sharks

Today was soooo busy. A big ~~shole~~ shoal of fish swam to Rocky Reef. Whenever that happens, loads of my shark cousins suddenly appear for a feast. The water swirls and churns as we swish and snap. We must be careful not to bite each other. Scary!

Wallis's mouth is so massive she could almost swallow me!

Bully's eyes are very small.

Bully the bull shark is just that - a real bully. He pushes small sharks like me out of the way. But when I grow up I'll be bigger than him, then I'll show him!

Most of the sharks around Rocky Reef are Caribbean reef sharks, like my friend Crib. She's not as big as us hammerheads, but she's a very fast hunter.

Crib is slim and streamlined.

Wallis is not only the biggest kind of shark - she's the biggest fish in the world. Luckily whale sharks like Wallis don't attack us. They feed like Manta, by filtering tiny creatures from the water.

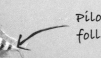
Pilot fish often follow sharks.

Whale Shark

Group Fish – Sharks

Adult length More than 12 metres

Weight Up to 20 tonnes

Habitat Warm seas and oceans

Food Small creatures such as shrimps, squid, young fish, plankton

Features Great size, huge mouth to suck in water, gills to sieve food

Tig eats anything, from jellyfish to turtles.

Tig's stripes fade with age.

Tig is one sneaky shark. He looks slow and lazy, then he suddenly attacks with great power. He's called a tiger shark because he has stripes like a tiger. At least, that's what Senior Shark says. I've never seen a tiger!

HURRICANE HITS ROCKY REEF

Giant waves smashed part of our reef

Yesterday's hurricane caused widespread damage along Rocky Reef. High winds whipped up huge waves that cracked corals, broke boulders and splintered stones. Reporter Barry Barracuda says: "I counted more than 100 injured fish, 200 lost shellfish and 250 homeless crabs. The corals will take 50 years to grow again. It's a heartbreaking sight."

Swept Away

What a night! I was deafened by the noise of the waves pounding Rocky Reef. Massive currents swept me away to a place called The River. There are strange creatures here I haven't seen before, but I've heard stories about them.

I don't like The River. Not enough salt.

The salmon are trying to get to Wide-Open Ocean to breed.

These fish say they are called salmon. They look really tasty, but they're too busy to be eaten. They can swim in rivers or the sea.

This guy looks seriously fierce. Al the American Alligator hates the sea's salty water. The storm surge carried him out there and he swam back here to The River as fast as he could!

Al paddles with legs. Wish I had legs!

Did you ever see such a ~~bizzar~~ ~~bazaar~~ bizarre fish as Snout the sawfish? Like Manta, she's a ray - a relative of mine. Sharks and rays have skeletons made of cartilage, not bone like most other fish.

Look at Snout's awesome chain-saw nose!

Sawfish

Group Fish – Rays

Adult length Up to 7 metres

Weight 500 kilogrammes or more

Habitat Warmer rivers, lakes, lagoons, estuaries and shallow coastal waters of the Atlantic Ocean

Food Fish, crabs, shellfish, worms, shrimps, other animals

Features Long, flat, tooth-edged snout to stir up mud and sand for food, flattened body

Lucky Escapes

I escaped from The River and got back to Rocky Reef. But more disaster! A shoal of horrible boats came past dragging their nasty nets. I watched helplessly as Dolly the dolphin got stuck in one of them.

Dolly's sharp teeth cut through the cords.

I keep well clear of the nets.

Dolly looks like a fish on the outside, but she has warm blood and breathes air. She's a ~~mmamul~~ mammal. If she ran out of air, she could drown!

It's not just Air-Breathers who die in the nets. Many sharks do too. We must keep swimming, so that water moves past our gills, bringing oxygen, which all creatures need. No swim = no oxygen = no life.

We hate the killer boats.

It would have been sad if Dolly had died, but ... waste not want not, I'd have had a big feast! Luckily for Dolly, she managed to bite through the net, untangle herself and swim to the surface just in time. Gasp!

Dolly got her flipper tangled.

The nets should catch only fish like these.

Bottlenose Dolphin

Group	Mammals – Cetaceans (whales and dolphins)
Adult length	Up to 4 metres
Weight	500 kilogrammes or more
Habitat	Warm seas and oceans worldwide
Food	Fish, squid, shrimps, crabs, other animals
Features	Blowhole on top of head, sharp teeth

There are more and more of these fishing boats nowadays. Their nets catch so many fish that there aren't many left for bigger hunters like me. This leaves us hungry. Boo-hoo!

Summer School

Summer is coming and it's time for our annual journey to the Cool Zone. It takes a couple of weeks' hard swimming to get there. Senior Shark says this journey is called a migration but I call it Summer School. We travel in big groups called schools, and we do it every Summer.

The Shark Skills manual has vital migration information.

Senior Shark leads the way.

LET'S MIGRATE!
Hammerheads vs. Green Turtles

Sharks migrate quickly in groups on a direct path. The green turtle travels alone along a more random route, slowly but for longer. Also it lives much longer. So in a lifetime, it swims ten times farther than a hammerhead.

	SMOOTH HAMMERHEAD	GREEN TURTLE
YEARLY MIGRATION	400-700 kilometres	2000 kilometres
AVERAGE SWIM SPEED	4-6 km/h	3 km/h
LIFETIME TOTAL DISTANCE	15,000 kilometres	150,000 kilometres

We stay close together.

We head north, keeping shallow water on our left. We're very safe. No one dares attack hundreds of fierce hammerheads! We'll stay at the Cool Zone for a few months and then the school will head back home to The Bay.

22

Sometimes other migrating animals swim with us for a while, like Shelly the turtle. When we get to the Cool Zone we feast on fish, mainly small mackerel. There are millions and trillions of them there, which is why we migrate.

Green Turtle

Group Reptiles – turtles and tortoises

Adult length 1.5 metres

Flipper span 2 metres

Weight 250 kilogrammes or more

Habitat Warm seas and oceans

Food Sea grass, seaweeds, some small creatures

Features Hard shell, beaked mouth, flipper-shaped limbs protected by tough scales

Young sharks follow the older ones.

Shelly is slow but strong.

On the Hunt

I didn't eat much while swimming, so now I'm really hungry. Hey, here's a shoal of mackerel - I'll grab a few. I apologize first, of course. I don't like killing, but I must eat to survive. When we leave the Cool Zone and head back, our yearly migration will be over.

My Shark Skills manual gives the science behind my supersense.

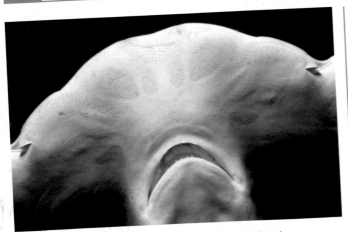

Human scientists call our pit-like sensors the ampullae of Lorenzini. Each of us has many thousands of them. Like smell and feeling, they work in cloudy water and at night. That's why sharks can hunt at almost any time. We're 24/7 predators!

ELECTROSENSORS

All sharks have tiny pits scattered over their head and front underside. These are sensitive to pulses of electricity sent out through the water by animal muscles.

Instructions for use

1. As you hunt, sweep your head from side to side, just above the ocean floor.
2. If your sensors pick up any electrical pulses, swim to where they feel strongest.
3. Turn in a small circle to feel where the electricity comes from and zero in.
4. Be ready – your victim may try and escape. Happy Hunting!

An old, slow fish that looks ill is just right for a bite-size snack. I can see it, smell it and feel the ripples it makes. I'll suddenly twist around and grab it. Sorry, little fish!

These fish are too quick for me to catch.

My victim – an old, slow fish.

This stingray's sting got stuck in my mouth for a week!

My last big meal was a delicious stingray. I'm ace at catching them. I swim just above the sea bed and when I detect electrical signals from animal muscles, my electrosensors tingle. I nose into the sand or mud and - result! I don't care about the sharp, jagged sting, or the strong venom it jabs in. I'm very tough!

Coral Island

On the way back from the Cool Zone, I stopped off at Coral Island. It's a colourful reef I visited once when I was little, for a holiday. It looks smaller now, but I'm much bigger!

The reef seems smaller and duller to me.

Queeny has lived on the Reef for 10 years.

Queeny the queen angelfish says the tiny coral creatures are like mini-flowers with stinging tentacles.

Corals grow in a-maze-ing shapes.

Barry Barracuda likes to holiday here, too.

Queeny says coral creatures, called polyps, make stony cup-shaped homes to protect their soft bodies. When they die, more polyps make homes on top, gradually building the huge reef.

But there are problems. Rivers bring water with horrible chemical pollution. Suzi Squid says it clogs her gills and stings her eyes. It also kills coral polyps, by making the water too warm and more acidic. Coral Island may be gone next time I pass by!

Polluted dead coral is pale or 'bleached'.

Reef fish are so bright. Imagine me in sunglasses ...

Suzi is a Caribbean reef squid.

White Fright!

This afternoon I swam past Broken Boulder to see if there was anything to eat. There was - me! White almost bit me in half! But it's all part of her job as a famous celebrity.

I used my head-lift to race upwards.

My muscles worked hard and fast.

I tail-swished as fast as I could.

Great White Shark

Group Fish – Sharks

Adult length 6 metres, perhaps more

Weight Over 1000 kilogrammes

Habitat Cool to warm waters worldwide

Food Animal prey from whales to seals, seabirds, turtles, and many kinds of fish and squid

Features Great size, razor-sharp teeth, massively powerful bite force

White's best trick is to swim up from the deep and take a massive bite from a victim like a sea lion. She finishes it off in a few gulps. What a superstar! Apparently she's been on television, and in movies and photos, more times than I've eaten cold dinners.

Today White's working for a human TV crew, to show how scientists study great white sharks. I suppose she deserves her fame. Senior Shark says she's the world's biggest hunting fish.

Human divers in a cage – cowards!

What a weird one-eyed shellfish!

White cleaned her huge sharp teeth for the show. Smile, please!

No other hunters make me feel scared. Apart from Bully and Tig. Also my close cousin Alexander the great hammerhead, who's bigger than me. That's definitely all. Oh, and Orca the killer whale, and ...

What They Say About Me

My diary describes what I think about all the creatures I meet.
But what do they think about me? Let's find out ...

> Hammerhead is OK, I suppose. The head shape's a bit weird, and the mouth quite small. But no one is as glamorous and good-looking as ME!

Great White Shark

Turtle

> I visit rarely, so I don't know much gossip. Hammerhead seems a nice shark, and has never tried to bite me. If that happened, I can turn fast and bite hard myself, y'know!

> I only saw that Hammerhead once, after the hurricane. Very caring, for a shark. Although I think if one salmon lagged behind, the shark would snap it up.

Sawfish

Manatee

> Dolphins and sharks have an uneasy relationship. We're alike in size, shape and the food we like. Yet we're so unlike in other ways. I breathe air. But if I had to like a shark, it'd be Hammerhead.

> Hammerhead protected me after the boating accident. Even with lots of blood in the water, other sharks kept away. But as we know, a shark can easily turn from friend to enemy.

Dolphin

Tricky Terms

Buoyancy Able to float on or rise up in water.

Camouflage Merging with the shapes, colours and patterns of the surroundings, to be less noticed.

Cartilage Lightweight, strong, smooth substance that is fairly stiff yet also bendy. It forms the skeletons of sharks and similar fish.

Current The movement or flow of water when a river flows into the sea, or sea water flows in with the tide.

Electrosensors Sensitive body parts that detect electrical currents passing through water, especially natural electrical pulses made by active animal muscles.

Mammal A warm-blooded animal that has fur or hair, an inner skeleton of bone, and feeds its young on mother's milk.

Mollusc A type of animal with a very flexible body, tentacles and perhaps a shell. Octopus, squid, shellfish such as conches and other seasnails, oysters, mussels and clams are all molluscs.

Oxygen An element that almost all living things must take in to stay alive. It is present in air and is dissolved in water.

Plankton Small living things that drift in water, rather than swim under their own power. Most are microscopic – too small to be seen with the unaided eye.

Rays Close relatives of sharks, with a flattened body and a flap-like 'wing' along each side, similar to skates.

Reef A large rocky structure at and/or just below sea level. Coral reefs are made by millions of tiny animals called coral polyps.

School A group of fish or similar water animals that stay close together and mostly move in the same direction, in a co-ordinated way, unlike a shoal.

Shellfish Water creatures with a hard outer shell for protection, such as whelks, conches, clams and limpets. Many shellfish belong to the mollusc group.

Shoal A group of fish or similar water animals that gather near each other in the same area, but swim about in different, random directions, unlike a school.

Skates Close relatives of sharks, with a flattened body and a flap-like 'wing' along each side, similar to rays.

Venom A harmful substance jabbed in with sharp body parts, such as teeth, spines or a sting, into a victim. Venom causes pain, inability to move or even death.

> Darling, I really don't take much notice of little creatures such as Hammerheads. Small animals are simply not very important. For me, bigger is better!

Whale Shark

Index